THE ESSENTIAL TRAITS OF A HAPPY AND GODLY WIFE

THE ESSENTIAL TRAITS OF A HAPPY AND GODLY WIFE

A Manual, Guide, and Resource
for Committed Women

David Scott, Ed.D., D.Min.

PCB

Published by Purple Chair Books and Educational Products, LLC

First Printing, 2025

Scott, David 1969-

The Essential Traits of a Happy and Godly Wife

By David Scott

ISBN: 978-1-953671-11-0

Self-Help/Inspirational

Printed in the United States of America

Interior designed by Md Al Amin (aminbookdesign@gmail.com)

Cover designed by Sadia A @sadia_coverz

Foreword

In every generation, God raises voices to call His daughters higher—not into perfection, but into purpose. *Essential Traits for a Happy Godly Wife* is more than a book; it is a sacred summons to rediscover the divine blueprint for womanhood, marriage, and legacy. In a world that often confuses beauty with worth and independence with isolation, this work reclaims the ancient truth: that joy, strength, and fulfillment are found not in striving, but in surrender to God's design.

This book is not a list of rules; it is an insight. It does not reduce a wife's role to household chores, nor does it idolize submission without understanding. Instead, it depicts a woman who is both caring and persistent, prayerful and strong, gentle yet rooted in truth. It reminds us that a godly wife is not a passive bystander in her husband's calling—she is a partner, a crown, a source of wisdom and grace who influences her home's environment and the path of future generations.

As a husband, father, pastor, or mentor, you will discover in these pages a guide to honor, uplift, and understand the women God has placed in your life. As a wife, mother, or woman of faith, you will find language for your longings, clarity for your calling, and strength for your seasons. Each trait explored here is not just a virtue to admire — it is a seed to nurture, a mirror to reflect, and a mantle to carry.

The Proverbs 31 woman is not a myth. She is not a relic of a bygone era. She is the woman who fears the Lord, builds her house with wisdom, speaks with kindness, and rises with purpose. She is the woman who prays in secret and leads with quiet strength. She is the woman whose joy is not dependent on circumstances but is covenantal— rooted in her relationship with the Lord and her commitment to walk in His ways.

This book is for the woman who desires more than just a happy marriage—she seeks a holy one. It is for the wife who yearns to be both treasured by her husband and accepted by her God. It is for the woman who knows that submission is not silence, but sacred alignment; that strength is not rebellion, but resilience wrapped in reverence.

To the reader: prepare to be challenged, encouraged, and transformed. Let these pages stir your spirit, renew your mind, and ignite your heart. Whether you are newly married, seasoned in your covenant, or preparing for the journey ahead, *Essential Traits for a Happy Godly Wife* will equip you to walk with grace, speak with wisdom, and love with eternity in view.

This is more than just a book. It is a legacy manual. Every woman who dares to live by these truths will not only be blessed by her children and praised by her husband, but she will also be celebrated in heaven as a faithful steward of her divine calling.

Let the journey begin.

— *Dr. David Scott, Ed.D., DMin.*
Pastor/Teacher/Theologian/Servant

Acknowledgements

To the love of my life, my number one fan, and my daily inspiration, the beautiful First Lady Tamara Scott a.k.a. (The Boss), and author of the fantastic women's devotional titled: *30 Days of Reflection from a Surrendered Heart.*

Table of Contents

Part I: Foundations of Godly Womanhood

Part II: Traits That Build a Joyful Marriage

Part III:
Traits That Multiply Legacy and Impact

Part IV:
Traits That Reflect Kingdom Authority

PART I:
FOUNDATIONS OF GODLY WOMANHOOD

Chapter 1

Rooted in Christ: The Source of True Joy

"You make known to me the path of life; in your presence there is fullness of joy; at your right hand are pleasures forevermore."
– *Psalm* 16:11 (ESV)

The Battle for Identity

In a world that shouts, "Be more! Do more! Prove your worth!" the spirit of a woman can become tired. Culture offers countless definitions of womanhood, each louder and more demanding than the last. The "perfect wife" is often portrayed as a flawless blend of beauty, ambition, sensuality, and independence. But these shifting standards are exhausting, and they rarely bring peace. The world presents carnal, challenging, and often unrealistic and self-serving ideas of what a woman should be.

The godly wife, however, is not shaped by the world's applause but by heaven's affirmation. Her identity is not based on her appearance, her productivity, or even her role as a wife—but on Christ alone. She is not defined by what she does, but by whose she is. A woman's most significant and highest aspect of beauty, femininity, and purpose is found in Christ and Him alone.

"For you died, and your life is now hidden with Christ in God."
– Colossians 3:3

When a woman is rooted in Christ, she no longer seeks approval—she lives from it. She no longer strives for validation. Instead, she rests in assurance. A woman who hides herself in Christ is whole, complete, and satisfied in Him. Her worth is not up for debate. It was settled at the cross. The woman who wraps herself in Christ, making Him her hiding place, her source of strength, and her source of contentment, is satisfied in Him. She would dare to profess that in Him she finds the fullness and completeness of joy. In Him, she finds identity.

Joy Is Not a Mood—It's a Manifestation

Joy is not the absence of hardship; it is the presence of God. It is not a fleeting emotion tied to circumstances, but a fruit of the Spirit born from intimacy with the Father.

"The joy of the Lord is your strength."
— Nehemiah 8:10

A wife rooted in Christ finds her joy not in her husband's mood, her children's actions, or her bank account—but in the wellspring of God's presence. Her joy is resilient. It is strengthened through worship, nourished by the Word, and grounded in eternity.

She laughs without fear of the future because she knows who holds it. She sings in the storm because she knows the One who walks on water. Her joy is not naive; it is prophetic. It declares, "God is good, even here."

The Fruit of Spiritual Intimacy

Joy is not created through effort. It is nurtured through intimacy. Just as a tree produces fruit by staying connected to its source, so a wife finds joy by remaining in Christ. Christ is the source of her strength, the source of her nourishment, and the water that allows and causes her to grow. Outside and away from Him, no woman can become or produce all that she was meant for. Unrooted in Christ, a woman lacks the source and the proper nourishment to grow a bounty of fruit.

"Abide in me, and I in you. As the branch cannot bear fruit by itself, unless it abides in the vine, neither can you, unless you abide in me."
— John 15:4

Spiritual intimacy is not reserved for the super-spiritual. It is the daily pursuit of God's presence—through prayer, worship, and the Word. It is choosing to sit at His feet before standing in the kitchen. It is whispering His name in the mundane moments. It is inviting Him into the laundry room, the carpool line, the budget meeting, and the bedroom.

The more a wife abides, the more she overflows. Her joy becomes contagious, her peace a refuge, and her presence a sanctuary.

From Performance to Presence

The culture says, "Do more." Christ says, "Come to Me." The culture says, "Be everything." Christ says, "I am your everything." The culture says, "Find yourself." Christ says, "Lose yourself in Me and you will find life."

Being a happy and godly wife isn't about checking off a list. It is about cultivating a heart that's rooted in Christ. It's about living from the inside out, not the outside in. It's about trading performance for presence and pressure for peace.

Legacy Reflection

A wife rooted in Christ becomes a source of joy for her home. Her laughter is sincere and sacred. Her peace is active and impactful. It is powerful. Her identity is genuine. It is bought with blood. No inconsistent and ever-changing trends can influence her. No, she is anchored in truth. She is not driven by fear. She is guided by faith. She is not frantically striving or trying to be enough. She turns and runs to her Lord. She knows Christ is more than enough. This is the beginning of her joy. This is the foundation of her legacy.

Reflection

"When God reveals the path of life, He doesn't just point the way—He walks it with you. In His presence, joy is not seasonal—it's sovereign. And at His right hand, pleasure isn't fleeting; it is eternal. This is not just a promise—it's a positioning."

Chapter 2

The Power of Submission: Strength in Surrender

"Wives, submit yourselves unto your own husbands, as unto the Lord."
– Ephesians 5:22 (KJV)

Submission Misunderstood

Few words in modern discourse generate more discomfort than "submission." For many, the idea of submission evokes images of silence, suppression, or servitude. However, this should not be the case. In the mind of a great and sovereign God, nothing could be further from the truth. Biblical submission is not about losing your voice. It is about gaining divine alignment. In no way is it about weakness. On the contrary, it is about wisdom. It is not oppression. It is about orchestration.

Submission, in the Father's kingdom, is not about inferiority. It is about order. God is a God of divine design, and within marriage, He has established a rhythm and flow that reflects heaven's harmony. When a wife submits to her husband "as unto the Lord," she is not bowing to a man—she is yielding to God's blueprint, manual, and design.

"But I want you to understand that the head of every man is Christ, the head of a wife is her husband, and the head of Christ is God."
– 1 Corinthians 11:3 (ESV)

This divine order is not a hierarchy of value—it is a flow of responsibility. Christ submitted to the Father, yet He was fully and wholly God. Submission does not diminish identity. On the contrary, it reveals maturity.

Redefining Biblical Submission

Biblical submission is not passive; it is powerful. It is a deliberate and intentional choice to honor, support, and follow God's design for leadership in the home. Clearly, submission is not about blind obedience. Instead, it involves spiritual discernment. A godly wife submits not because she is forced, but because she is free.

Submission in marriage is not silence; rather, it is a strategic agreement. It represents the stance of a woman who understands her influence is at its strongest when her spirit is surrendered. Her submission does not mean giving up, abandoning, or losing herself; instead, it involves releasing her capacity and potential to fulfill the purpose to which she was called. She does not compete with her husband. Instead, she completes him.

"She opens her mouth with wisdom,
and the teaching of kindness is on her tongue."
– Proverbs 31:26

A submissive wife is not a doormat—she is a doorway. Her humility invites heaven's favor. Her honor unlocks her husband's potential. Her surrender becomes her strength.

Mutual Honor and Divine Order

In marriage, submission is mutual, not one-sided. The writer of Ephesians 5:21 sets the tone: "*Submit to one another out of reverence for Christ.*" Before the apostle Paul talks to wives, he calls both spouses to mutual submission—an environment of respect, humility, and spiritual covering.

A godly husband does not dominate. Instead, he leads with love. He does not demand submission. On the contrary, he earns it through sacrifice. Just as Christ laid down His life for the church, a husband sets aside his pride, preferences, and comfort for his wife's growth.

"Husbands, love your wives, just as Christ loved
the church and gave himself up for her."
– Ephesians 5:25

When both husband and wife act and walk with mutual respect, submission becomes a partnership—not a dictatorship. The wife supports her husband's leadership, and the husband follows Christ. The home becomes a sanctuary of divine order, where peace prevails and purpose grows.

The Strength of Surrender

Submission is not a lack of strength; it is the guiding of it. A wife who submits does not diminish herself; she shines brighter. Her surrender is not to the unpredictable wishes and imaginations of men, but to God's wisdom. She is not losing herself; she is discovering her greatest purpose.

In surrender, she finds clarity. In honor, she gains influence. In alignment, she earns authority. Through her choice and willing surrender, she becomes a crown to her husband, a pillar in her home, and a reflection of Christ's beauty.

"A *wife of noble character is her husband's crown...*"
– Proverbs 12:4a

Legacy Reflection

The power of submission comes from trust, not control. It is the sacred strength of a woman who recognizes her worth, walks in wisdom, and chooses God's way over the world's noise. The woman who surrenders is not silenced—she is sanctified. She is not oppressed; she is ordained. She is not beneath. Instead, she stands beside her partner, building with grace and glory. This is the strength of surrender. This is the power of submission. This is the legacy of a happy and godly wife.

Reflection

"Submission in marriage is not surrender to man—it is surrender to divine order. When a wife honors her husband as unto the Lord, she doesn't lose her voice—she amplifies heaven's harmony in the home."

Chapter 3

A Heart of Worship: Living for an Audience of One

"Yet a time is coming and has now come when the true worshipers will worship the Father in spirit and truth, for they are the kind of worshipers the Father seeks."
— John 4:23 (NIV)

Worship Is Not a Sound—It's a Surrender

In a world fixated on performance, applause, and visibility, the godly wife chooses a different stage. She lives before an audience of One. Her worship is not limited to Sunday services or music playlists. It is the posture of her heart, the rhythm of her life, and the fragrance of her surrender.

Regarding the godly woman, worship is not only what she sings; it is how she serves. It is not only what she feels. It is how she fights. It is not just what she does; it is who she becomes.

"Therefore, I urge you... to offer your bodies as a living sacrifice, holy and pleasing to God—this is your true and proper worship."
— Romans 12:1

Daily Devotion: The Altar of Intimacy

A heart of worship is developed in the secret place. It is anchored not on emotion but on consistency. Daily devotion serves as the altar where intimacy is created. It is where the godly wife encounters her King—not to check a box but to be transformed.

She opens her Bible not just for information, but for revelation. She prays not just to perform, but to connect. She writes in her journals not to vent, but to listen. Her mornings are unhurried. They are sacred. Her evenings are not wasted; they are filled with reflection.

"In the morning, O Lord, You will hear my voice; in the morning I will order my prayer to You and eagerly watch."
— Psalm 5:3

Daily devotion is not legalism. It is life. It is oxygen for her spirit, the oil in her lamp, and the anchor of her soul.

Praise: The Sound of Victory

Praise is not just a reaction; it is the most potent of weapons. It signifies faith rising above confusion, doubt, and fear. It proclaims truth in defiance of lies. It is the melody of heaven breaking into earth.

When the godly wife praises, not only does she bombard the throne and presence of God, but she shifts the atmosphere. Her praise silences anxiety. Not only does she confuse the adversary's plans, but she also confounds the enemy. She invites the presence of God into her home, her marriage, and her mind.

"Let the high praises of God be in their mouth, and a two-edged sword in their hand."
— Psalm 149:6

Praise is not only for good days; it is essential for battle days. Praise is evident in how she fights for her family, breaks free, and achieves success without exhaustion, fatigue, or overexertion.

Worship as Warfare and Renewal

Worship is active, not passive; it is powerful. It is how the godly wife fights in the spirit. When she worships, she proclaims that God is greater than her circumstances, stronger than her fears, and faithful through every season. She declares that God is more than capable of doing exceedingly above and beyond all she might hope for or imagine. In worship, she praises God in advance for what He plans to do. Worship demolishes strongholds. It restores perspective. It renews strength.

"But those who wait on the Lord shall renew their strength; they shall mount up with wings like eagles..."
— Isaiah 40:31

In worship, she lays down her burdens and picks up His peace. She exchanges weariness for wonder. She trades confusion for clarity. She is not escaping reality—she is engaging eternity.

Living for an Audience of One

The godly wife does not worship for approval, applause, or validation. She worships because He is worthy. Her life is not a performance; it is a sacrifice. Her joy does not come from being seen, but from being genuinely and authentically known.

The godly wife worships while folding laundry, driving to work, and praying for her children. Her life is a sanctuary; her heart is an altar.

"Whatever you do, work at it with all your heart, as working for the Lord, not for human masters."
— Colossians 3:23

She does not need a stage; she has a Savior. She does not need a crowd; she has a calling. She does not need approval; she has anointing.

Legacy Reflection

A heart of worship is the foundation of a godly wife's strength. It is her source of joy, the secret to her peace, and her strategy in warfare. She is not just a wife; she is a worshipper. She is not just a homemaker; she is a history maker. She is not just surviving; she is surrendering, singing, and soaring. This is her power. This is her posture. This is her legacy.

Reflection

"True worship isn't a performance—it's a posture. When spirit and truth converge, heaven doesn't just listen—it responds. The Father isn't seeking noise—He's seeking alignment."

Chapter 4

The Beauty of Holiness: Set Apart for Glory

"Worship the Lord in the beauty of holiness;
tremble before Him, all the earth."
— Psalm 96:9 (KJV)

Holiness Is Not Legalism—It's Legacy

In a culture that values compromise, the godly wife chooses consecration. She is the kind of woman who is not driven by trends. Instead, she is guided by truth. For the godly woman, holiness is not a burden she carries. It is a beauty she wears. Holiness is not a list of restrictions, but it is a lifestyle of revelation.

To be holy means to be consecrated and set apart, marked by heaven, reserved for glory. Holiness is not perfection. Instead, it is a pursuit. It is the daily choice to reflect the character of Christ in thought, speech, and lifestyle.

"But just as He who called you is holy, so be holy in all you do."
— 1 Peter 1:15

Holiness is not outdated; it is eternal. It is not unattractive; instead, it is irresistible to heaven. It is not weakness; it's warfare.

Purity in Thought: Guarding the Inner Sanctuary

The battleground of holiness begins in the mind. All battles and wars start, are fought, and are won in the mind. The godly wife understands that her thoughts shape her environment. She does not dwell on bitterness, lust, or comparison—she renews her mind daily with the Word of God.

"Do not be conformed to this world,
but be transformed by the renewing of your mind..."
— Romans 12:2

The godly woman guards her imagination like a sacred garden. She refuses to rehearse offense, replay temptation, or dwell in fear. Intentionally, her thoughts are not random; they are redeemed. Purity in thought is not passive; it is intentional. It is choosing truth over lies, faith over fear, and grace over gossip.

Purity in Speech: Words That Build and Bless

The godly wife understands that her words hold significance. She does not speak thoughtlessly. On the contrary, she speaks prophetically. Her tongue is not a weapon of harm—it is a tool of building up.

"Let no corrupt communication proceed out of your mouth, but
that which is good to the use of edifying..."
— Ephesians 4:29

She avoids gossip, slander, and manipulation. Instead, she intentionally speaks life over her husband, children, and home. Her words are filled with grace, guided by wisdom, and rooted in truth. Purity in speech doesn't mean silence; it means sanctification. It's choosing to speak words that heal rather than harm. She understands that her words have the power to heal, give life, or tear down and destroy.

Purity in Lifestyle: Living Set Apart

Holiness is not just what she believes; it is how she acts. The godly wife lives with integrity, humility, and purpose. Her choices reflect her calling. Her habits embody her hope. She does not dress to seduce. She dresses to honor. She does not entertain what defiles. She seeks what sanctifies. Her lifestyle is not a response to culture; it reflects covenant.

"Come out from among them and be separate," says the Lord. Touch no unclean thing, and I will receive you."
— 2 Corinthians 6:17

Purity in lifestyle is not isolation; it is illumination. She is a light in the darkness, a standard in the storm, and a sanctuary in chaos.

Holiness as Attraction and Protection

Holiness is more than a shield—it is a sign. It draws heaven's favor, angelic protection, and divine alignment. The godly wife who walks in holiness becomes a magnet for miracles, a vessel of virtue, and a carrier of glory. As a woman confident of her purpose, calling, and destiny, she anticipates God's protection, favor, and provision in every situation and circumstance. Holiness protects her marriage from compromise. It shields her children from confusion. It guards her heart from deception.

"He who walks uprightly walks securely..."
— Proverbs 10:9

Holiness is not just about what she avoids; it is about what she carries. She carries peace, purity, and power. She's not just admired. She is anointed.

Legacy Reflection

The beauty of holiness is not found in rules. It is in radiance. The glow of a woman who walks with God, speaks with grace, and lives with conviction. She is not common. She is consecrated. She is not trendy. On the contrary, she is timeless. She does not blend in. She stands out boldly. This is her protection, her attraction, her legacy.

Reflection

“Worship isn’t just a sound—it’s a sanctified stance. When holiness becomes beautiful to us, trembling becomes natural before Him. The earth doesn’t shake because it’s afraid—it shakes because it recognizes glory.”

Chapter 5

Faith-Filled Living: Trusting God in Every Season

"Trust in the Lord with all your heart and lean not on your own understanding; in all your ways submit to Him, and He will make your paths straight."
— Proverbs 3:5–6 (NIV)

Seasons Change—God Doesn't

Life is a tapestry of seasons. Some are bright with blessings; others are shadowed by uncertainty. The godly wife learns to trust not in the season but in the Savior. Her faith is not seasonal. Instead, it is steadfast. Her peace is not circumstantial. It is supernatural.

Faith-filled living does not deny reality; it trusts in divinity. It is the sacred choice to believe that God is good, even amidst life's hardships. It reflects the attitude of a woman who walks through valleys with clarity and storms with song.

"Even though I walk through the valley of the shadow of death, I will fear no evil, for You are with me..."
— Psalm 23:4

She remains calm. She prays. She stays steady. She rests. She does not fall apart. She clings.

Navigating Uncertainty with Peace

Uncertainty is not lacking direction. It is the call to deeper trust. The godly wife does not need every answer. She trusts the One who has them. Her peace does not rest in clarity. It is in intimacy.

"You will keep in perfect peace those whose minds are steadfast, because they trust in You."
— Isaiah 26:3

She anchors her soul in scripture. She silences fear through worship. She surrounds herself with truth-tellers, not fear-mongers. Her home becomes a sanctuary of peace, not a storm of stress. Living with faith means choosing peace over panic, prayer over pressure, and praise over pessimism.

Testimonies of Provision and Breakthrough

Faith is not just a theory. It is testimony. The godly wife shares stories of God's provision, protection, and power. She remembers the times He provided when the account was empty. She recalls the healing when the diagnosis was grim. She celebrates the restoration when the relationship seemed broken.

"I was young and now I am old, yet I have never seen the righteous forsaken or their children begging bread."
— Psalm 37:25

Her faith is tangible, rooted in experience. She has seen God move mountains, open wombs, cancel debts, and restore joy. Her testimony becomes her lesson, and her breakthrough shapes her plan. She shares her story not to boast, but to build up others. She becomes a living altar of remembrance, a walking witness of God's faithfulness.

Trusting God in Every Season

Spring brings new beginnings. Summer yields abundance. Autumn marks a transition. Winter provides stillness. Yet, in every season, God remains constant. The godly wife learns to trust Him through the process of planting, pruning, waiting, and harvesting. She does not rush the process. She respects it. She does not resent the silence. She embraces it.

"There is a time for everything,
and a season for every activity under the heavens."
— Ecclesiastes 3:1

Faith-filled living is not just seasonal obedience; it is a lifelong surrender. It means trusting God both when doors open and when they close. It involves praising Him, whether the answer is "yes" or "not yet."

Legacy Reflection

Faith-filled living is the legacy of a godly wife. It symbolizes the aroma of her trust, the power of her surrender, and the testimony of her trials. She remains unshaken. She is secure. She is not uncertain. She is grounded. She is not merely surviving; she is soaring. Her faith is not fragile; it is fierce. Her peace is not passive; it is prophetic. Her life is not random; it is redeemed. This is her strength. This is her story. This is her season.

Reflection

“Trust isn’t passive—it’s prophetic. When you lean not on logic but on the Lord, you don’t just walk—you align. Submission isn’t a weakness; it’s the GPS of destiny. And when God directs, crooked becomes straight, delay becomes divine, and every step becomes sacred.”

PART II:
TRAITS THAT BUILD A JOYFUL MARRIAGE

Chapter 6

Respect and Reverence: Honoring Your Husband's Role

"Let the wife see that she respects her husband."
— Ephesians 5:33 (ESV)

Respect Is Not Optional—It's Ordained

In a culture that prizes independence, honoring a husband's role may seem old-fashioned. Yet in God's kingdom, respect is strategic and reflects alignment with divine design, not weakness or submission to ego.

Respect is not something you earn. On the contrary, it is something you give. It is not based on perfection. It is based on position. When a wife honors her husband, she celebrates the God who appointed him as the head of the home. She does not worship him—she respects the role he holds.

"The head of every man is Christ, the head of a wife is her husband, and the head of Christ is God."
— 1 Corinthians 11:3

This divine order is not about control. It is about covering. Respect becomes the shield that guards marriage, the oil that softens conflict, and the key that unlocks leadership.

Speaking Life: The Power of Affirmation

Words create worlds. The godly wife knows that her tongue is more than a tool. It is a torch. She has the power to ignite confidence or insecurity, courage or confusion, strength or shame.

"*The tongue has the power of life and death...*"
— Proverbs 18:21

She speaks positively, supports her husband's leadership as he develops, celebrates his efforts, builds him up, and offers affirmation without comparison.

Her words become prophetic seeds. She says, "I believe in you," and heaven echoes, "So do I." She says, "You're a man of wisdom," and the Spirit begins to stir wisdom within him. Her affirmation is not flattery—it is faith in action.

"A *wise woman builds her house...*"
— Proverbs 14:1a

She fosters with praise, not pressure. She empowers with honor, not harshness. Her voice becomes a sanctuary, not a storm.

Respect as a Spiritual Weapon

Respect is active and transformative. It spreads pride, reduces division, and can turn conflict into resolution, especially when chosen during challenging moments. Respect is not about agreeing on everything. It is about aligning with God's heart. It involves choosing to honor even when feelings try to lead to dishonor. It means seeing others through the eyes of heaven, not through the lens of frustration.

"A *gentle and quiet spirit... is of great worth in God's sight.*"
— 1 Peter 3:4

Respect is not weakness — it is strength. It silences the enemy's accusations. It breaks generational cycles of dishonor. It models kingdom culture amid chaos.

When a wife respects her husband, it fosters a positive home environment. Leadership can be developed rather than restrained, and marriage can be understood as a partnership rather than merely an agreement.

Honoring the Role, Not Idolizing the Man

Respect involves honoring others despite their imperfections. A committed wife recognizes her husband's flaws but values his essential role, supports him through prayer, and encourages his growth rather than enabling unhealthy behavior. She honors the mantle, even when the man is still growing. She reveres the calling, even when the character is being developed. Her respect becomes a mirror reflecting who he is becoming in Christ.

> *"Encourage one another and build each other up..."*
> – 1 Thessalonians 5:11

Her respect is not blind. It is courageous. It looks past the present and focuses on the mission.

Legacy Reflection

Respect and reverence are still considered essential qualities by some people. These traits are often linked to an understanding of relationships, spiritual beliefs, and communication. She is not a critic—she is a crown. She is not a rival—she is a refuge. She is not a burden, but a builder. Her respect is not weakness; it is strength. Her reverence is not silence; it is strategy. Her honor is not submission to man—it is surrender to God. This is her power. This is her stance. This is her legacy.

Reflection

"Respect isn't a reward—it's a revelation. When a wife sees her husband through heaven's lens, she doesn't just honor the man—she activates the mantle. In kingdom marriage, respect builds the throne where love and leadership can dwell."

Chapter 7

Gentleness and Grace: The Strength of Softness

"*Let your gentleness be evident to all. The Lord is near.*"
— Philippians 4:5 (NIV)

Softness Is Not Weakness—It's Wisdom

In a world that links strength to loudness and dominance, the godly wife discovers a deeper power: gentleness. Her gentleness is not a sign of weakness. It signifies spiritual growth. Her elegance isn't just passivity—it shows prophetic self-control. She doesn't need to raise her voice to be heard—her spirit resonates louder than her words.

Gentleness does not mean lacking conviction. On the contrary, it signifies having control. It reflects a woman who has mastered her emotions rather than suppressing them. It characterizes a wife who understands that her strength lies in revealing herself rather than reacting impulsively.

"*A gentle tongue is a tree of life,*
but perverseness in it breaks the spirit."
— Proverbs 15:4

She does not use her words to wound or hurt. Instead, she uses them to nurture. She does not weaponize her emotions. She sanctifies them.

Emotional Intelligence and Tone: The Language of Love

Tone acts as the thermostat of the home. The godly wife understands that her words are often more potent than her actions. Her emotional intelligence enables her to discern timing, temperature, and tenderness.

She does not respond with anger. She communicates with wisdom. She does not escalate conflict. She diffuses it with grace. Her tone is not sharp. On the contrary, it is soothing. Her presence does not provoke. Instead, it brings peace.

"*A gentle answer turns away wrath,*
but a harsh word stirs up anger."
– Proverbs 15:1

Emotional intelligence means understanding emotions, responding thoughtfully, and showing compassion. It is about discerning when to speak, listen, remain silent, or pray. A godly wife does not avoid conflict. She handles it with wisdom. Her tone becomes a means of healing rather than hostility.

Grace in Conflict and Correction

Grace is not the absence of truth. It is the environment in which truth is received. The godly wife does not shy away from difficult conversations—she faces them with humility and respect. She corrects without condemning. She confronts without crushing.

"*Brothers and sisters, if someone is caught in a sin, you who live by the Spirit should restore that person gently.*"
– Galatians 6:1

Grace in conflict involves choosing restoration over retaliation. It means asking, "How can I heal this?" instead of "How can I win this?" It means seeing the person, not just the problem.

In correction, she does not shame—she guides. She does not expose—she builds up. Her words are not daggers—they are balm.

Grace is a strategic approach rather than a sign of weakness. It neutralizes pride, reduces defensiveness, and fosters open, constructive dialogue.

The Strength of Softness

Gentleness is not about lacking boundaries. It is about embodying beauty. It is the strength to remain calm amid chaos, the power to love despite offense, and the wisdom to wait when impulse urges a response.

The godly wife who walks in gentleness and grace becomes a sanctuary in her home. Her presence brings peace. Her words bring healing. Her spirit brings safety.

> *"She opens her mouth with wisdom,*
> *and the teaching of kindness is on her tongue."*
> – Proverbs 31:26

She is not loud, she is luminous. She is not forceful; she is faithful. She is not abrasive; she is anointed. Her softness is not weakness; it's warfare. Her grace is not silence—it's strategy. Her gentleness is not retreat—it's revelation.

Legacy Reflection

Gentleness and grace are the heritage of a godly wife. They are the aroma of her faith, the strength of her spirit, and the wisdom in her walk. She does not control. She elevates. She does not demand. She perceives. She does not destroy. She mentors. This is her power. This is her stance. This is her legacy.

Reflection

"Gentleness isn't weakness—it's kingdom strength under control. When your spirit stays calm and your character stays kind, heaven draws near. The Lord doesn't just visit gentleness—He dwells in it."

Chapter 8

Wisdom in Speech: The Art of Godly Communication

"The wise woman builds her house,
but with her own hands the foolish one tears hers down."
— Proverbs 14:1 (NIV)

Words Build or Break

Speech is inherently spiritual, not neutral. Each word spoken holds power, either uplifting or damaging. The godly wife recognizes that her voice goes beyond mere hearing—it impacts how others feel. Her words help create the home's atmosphere, boost her husband's confidence, and nurture her children's emotional security.

Godly communication is not just about what is said, but about how, when, and why it is said. Wisdom in speech involves speaking truth gently, offering correction with compassion, and expressing conviction calmly.

"The tongue has the power of life and death, and those who love it will eat its fruit."
— Proverbs 18:21

She does not speak to dominate, but to make disciples. She does not use her voice to control, but to nurture.

Avoiding Nagging, Sarcasm, and Strife

Nagging is not persistence. On the contrary, it is pressure. It undermines trust, fosters resentment, and shows a lack of faith in God's timing. The godly wife does not repeat demands. She releases them in prayer. She does not manipulate. She ministers with silence when needed.

> "*Better to live on a corner of the roof*
> *than share a house with a quarrelsome wife.*"
> – Proverbs 21:9

Sarcasm is not humor. On the contrary, it is hostility in disguise. It hurts with wit and hides criticism in comedy. The godly wife prefers sincerity over snark, clarity over cleverness, and kindness over harsh remarks.

Strife is not a sign of strength. It is spiritual undermining. It creates division, reduces peace, and opens the door for negativity. A godly wife doesn't incite conflict—instead, she brings calm to chaos.

> "*A gentle answer turns away wrath, but a harsh word stirs up anger.*"
> – Proverbs 15:1

She does not weaponize her words—she worships with them.

Speaking with Discernment and Timing

Discernment is knowing what to say. Timing is knowing when to say it. The godly wife understands that even truth spoken out of season can feel like betrayal. She waits on the Holy Spirit before she speaks. She listens more than she lectures. She prays before she presses.

> "*There is a time to be silent and a time to speak.*"
> – Ecclesiastes 3:7

She does not rush to rebuke. She rests in revelation. She does not speak to prove she's right. On the contrary, if she speaks at all, she speaks to be righteous. Her words are seasoned with grace, not overwhelmed by emotion.

Discernment is not silence. It is a strategy. It is a skill to recognize when a heart is open, when a moment is sacred, and when a word can heal rather than harm.

The Ministry of Words

The godly wife views her speech as a form of ministry. Her words are purposeful; they are redemptive. She speaks life into her husband's identity, her children's future, and her home's environment. She declares promises, not problems. She proclaims and prophesies peace, not panic. She speaks with the authority of heaven and the tenderness of Christ.

"She opens her mouth with wisdom,
and the teaching of kindness is on her tongue."
– Proverbs 31:26

Her voice becomes a sanctuary. Her tone becomes a balm. Her speech becomes a seed of legacy.

Legacy Reflection

Wisdom in speech reflects the legacy of a godly wife. It is the fragrance of her faith, the proof of her maturity, and the overflow of her closeness with God. She does not nag—she nurtures. She does not mock, but ministers. She does not provoke, but she protects. Her words are not loud; they are luminous. Her tone is not sharp. It is sacred. Her speech is not careless; it is consecrated. This is her power. This is her posture. This is her legacy.

Reflection

"A wise woman doesn't just decorate her house—she designs destiny. Her words frame the walls, her prayers lay the foundation, and her honor holds the roof in place. But when wisdom is absent, even her own hands become demolition tools."

Chapter 9

Hospitality and Warmth: Creating a Kingdom Atmosphere

"Do not forget to show hospitality to strangers, for by so doing some people have shown hospitality to angels without knowing it."
— Hebrews 13:2 (NIV)

Home as a Haven, Not Just a House

A godly wife understands that her home is more than just walls and furniture — it is a sanctuary. Her living room becomes a place of peace, her kitchen a table of fellowship, and her presence a refuge for weary hearts. She understands that hospitality is not about perfection. It is about presence. It is not about having the best décor. On the contrary, it is about creating an atmosphere where people feel seen, safe, and strengthened. The godly wife makes her home a haven by cultivating warmth, order, and spiritual sensitivity.

"She watches over the affairs of her household and does not eat the bread of idleness."
— Proverbs 31:27

She does not wait for guests to arrive to create peace. She builds it daily. Her home is not just clean. It is sacred and consecrated. Her hospitality is not just social, but spiritual.

The Ministry of Warmth

Warmth is not just a temperature; it is a tone. It is how a godly wife greets her husband at the door, listens to her children's stories, and welcomes guests with joy. Her smile is a sermon. Her embrace is a healing balm. Her demeanor opens the door to divine encounters. Warmth is not a sign of weakness; rather, it is a strategy to fight isolation, rejection, and fear. It reduces defensiveness and encourages connection. It embodies the fragrance of Christ in everyday interactions.

"Above all, love each other deeply, because love covers over a multitude of sins. Offer hospitality to one another without grumbling."
— 1 Peter 4:8–9

She does not host out of obligation. She hosts from abundance. Her warmth is not forced. It originates from a hidden place.

Hosting with Joy and Generosity

Hospitality is not just about entertaining. It is about embracing and welcoming others. The godly wife hosts joyfully, without stress. She opens her home generously, avoiding comparisons. She does not perform for show. Instead, she offers sincere hospitality. She does not try to impress. Her goal is to share and nurture. Her table is not just for meals. It is for service and ministry. Her living room is not just for comfort, but for inspiring and transformational conversation. Her home becomes a hub of healing, laughter, and legacy.

"Share with the Lord's people who are in need. Practice hospitality."
— Romans 12:13

A godly wife gives without counting. She serves without complaints. She hosts without hesitation. Her kindness is not measured by what she has, but by how willing she is to give. Whether it is a neighbor in need, a couple in trouble, or a friend passing through, she opens her door and her heart.

Creating a Kingdom Atmosphere

Candles and music do not create a kingdom atmosphere. It is cultivated through prayer and presence. The godly wife invites the Holy Spirit into her home daily. She consecrates and anoints her doorposts with peace. She fills her rooms with worship. She speaks life in every corner. Her home becomes a place where burdens are lifted, joy returns, and hearts are revived. Children feel safe. Husbands feel honored. Guests feel loved. The atmosphere shifts because the Spirit reigns.

"Blessed are those who dwell in Your house;
they are ever praising You."
— Psalm 84:4

She does not just decorate; she sanctifies. She does not just host; she heals. Her home becomes a kingdom embassy, a place where heaven touches earth.

Legacy Reflection

Hospitality and warmth are the legacy of a godly wife. They are the fragrance of her faith, the rhythm of her generosity, and the ministry of her presence. She is not just a hostess; she is a healer. She is not just a homemaker; she is a history maker. She is not just serving food; she is serving faith. Her home is not just a place; it is a portal. Her warmth is not just emotional; it is eternal. Her hospitality is not just cultural but kingdom-driven. This is her power. This is her posture. This is her legacy.

Reflection

"Hospitality isn't just kindness—it's kingdom discernment in disguise. Every open door is a potential altar, and every stranger might carry heaven's assignment. When you host with honor, you don't just serve people—you entertain the presence of God."

Chapter 10

Forgiveness and Mercy: Healing Through Humility

"Be kind and compassionate to one another,
forgiving each other, just as in Christ God forgave you."
– Ephesians 4:32 (NIV)

Offense Is a Trap—Forgiveness Is a Key

Offense is subtle. It creeps in through unmet expectations, careless words, and unresolved wounds. If left unchecked, it hardens the heart, poisons the atmosphere, and damages trust. The godly wife understands that offense is not just emotional but also spiritual. It is a trap designed to steal peace, distort perspective, and block blessings. Forgiveness is not a feeling; it is a decision. It is the sacred choice to release what happened, not because it was right, but because God is righteous. It is not forgetting; it is freeing. It is not a sign of weakness; it is a form of warfare.

"A person's wisdom yields patience;
it is to one's glory to overlook an offense."
– Proverbs 19:11

Letting go of offense is not denial, but liberation. It involves choosing healing over bitterness, peace over pride, and restoration over retaliation.

Mercy: The Ministry of Heaven

Mercy is more than a virtue. It is a call. It embodies God's heart, expressed through His daughters. The godly wife doesn't demand flawlessness; she offers grace. She does not keep score. She covers with compassion.

"Blessed are the merciful, for they will be shown mercy."
— Matthew 5:7

Mercy does not allow dysfunction. Instead, it fosters redemption. It looks past the current moment to see the miracle. It does not justify sin; instead, it encourages transformation. When a wife embodies mercy, she reflects Christ. Her home becomes a sanctuary of healing, and her marriage serves as a testament to grace.

Reconciliation as Ministry

Reconciliation is more than just resolving issues. It involves restoration. It is the act of bringing hearts back into harmony with heaven and each other. The godly wife recognizes that every act of forgiveness is a prophetic statement: "God still heals. God still restores. God still reigns."

"All this is from God, who reconciled us to Himself through Christ and gave us the ministry of reconciliation."
— 2 Corinthians 5:18

Reconciliation demands humility. It involves setting aside the need to be right to be truly righteous. It means choosing unity over ego, peace over pride, and love over logic. The godly wife becomes a bridge, not a barrier. She initiates healing conversations. She prays before she responds. She listens with her heart, not just her ears.

Reconciliation is not a sign of weakness—it is a fight against division. It is the act of repairing what the enemy has tried to destroy.

Healing Through Humility

Humility is the foundation where healing begins. It is the stance of a woman who recognizes that her strength comes from surrender. She does not boast of herself. Instead, she lifts Christ. She does not protect her pride—she guards her peace.

"Humble yourselves before the Lord, and He will lift you up."
— James 4:10

Healing through humility involves saying, "I was wrong." It means asking, "Will you forgive me?" It consists of choosing vulnerability over vengeance. The godly wife does not wait for the other person to change—she becomes the change. Her humility acts as a healing balm. Her mercy becomes a ministry. Her forgiveness leaves a legacy.

Legacy Reflection

Forgiveness and mercy are the legacy of a godly wife. They are the fragrance of her faith, the evidence of her maturity, and the ministry of her heart. She does not hold grudges; she has grace. She does not rehearse offenses—she releases them. She does not demand justice; she offers mercy. Her humility heals. Her mercy mends. Her forgiveness sets her free. This is her power. This is her posture. This is her legacy.

Reflection

"Kindness is not optional—it's kingdom currency. Compassion is not weakness—it's warfare against bitterness. And forgiveness isn't forgetting—it's remembering the cross and choosing to build what Christ already redeemed."

PART III:
TRAITS THAT MULTIPLY LEGACY AND IMPACT

Chapter 11

Diligence and Stewardship: Managing Well What God Entrusts

"Moreover, it is required in stewards that one be found faithful."
— 1 Corinthians 4:2 (NKJV)

Stewardship Is Sacred

Everything we possess—our time, talents, finances, and homes—is not truly ours. It is entrusted to us by God. The godly wife recognizes that she is more than just a homemaker; she is a steward of heaven's resources. Her diligence is not motivated by duty but by devotion. Stewardship is not about ownership; it is about obedience. It is the sacred responsibility to manage what God has entrusted to her with excellence, integrity, and purpose.

"The earth is the Lord's, and everything in it,
the world, and all who live in it."
— Psalm 24:1

She does not waste what God has given. She multiplies it. She does not hoard—she honors. She does not operate in lack—she lives in alignment.

⌛ Time: The Currency of Eternity

Time isn't just a schedule; it's a seed. A wise and godly wife values and understands time by showing her true priorities, focusing on lasting purpose over constant busyness, and recognizing what matters most.

"Teach us to number our days,
that we may gain a heart of wisdom."
— Psalm 90:12

She starts her day with intention and ends it peacefully. Her plans are guided by prayer, making her schedule meaningful. She prioritizes devotion, family, and self-care through grace, not guilt. Time stewardship is not about doing more. It is about doing what matters most.

Money: A Tool, Not a Master

Money is not evil; it is a tool. The godly wife does not fear finances. She manages them with wisdom. She budgets transparently, gives joyfully, and saves intentionally. She recognizes that every dollar involves a choice, and each choice reflects trust.

"Honor the Lord with your wealth,
with the first fruits of all your crops."
— Proverbs 3:9

She tithes not out of obligation but from abundance. Her giving is generous. She understands that generosity invites supernatural provision. She avoids debt, practices discipline and teaches her children the value of contentment. Her financial stewardship is not about accumulation. Instead, it is about aligning with kingdom purpose.

Resource Wisdom: Multiplying What's in Her Hands

The godly wife multiplies. She takes what seems small and makes it sacred. She stretches meals, repurposes space, and turns ordinary moments into lasting impact. She is not wasteful. On the contrary, she is watchful.

"She considers a field and buys it;
out of her earnings she plants a vineyard."
— Proverbs 31:16

She is resourceful, creative, and strategic. She doesn't need anything extra to achieve more. She makes the most of what she already has. Her stewardship is not about striving; it is about surrendering her resources to the One who multiplies loaves and fish. She builds systems, not stress. She creates order, not overwhelm. She manages her home like a kingdom embassy—efficient, peaceful, and filled with purpose.

Productivity with Peace

Productivity in the kingdom isn't about hustle; it's about harmony. The godly wife doesn't chase burnout. Instead, she cultivates balance. She works diligently but also rests intentionally. She understands that peace isn't the absence of work; it's the presence of God within her work.

"In returning and rest you shall be saved;
in quietness and trust shall be your strength."
— Isaiah 30:15

Her to-do list does not define her identity. Her worth isn't based on her output. She is productive because she is grounded. She is fruitful because she is faithful. She doesn't strive; she resides. Her home moves to a rhythm, not a rush. Her days are guided by grace, not grind. Her diligence stems from devotion, not demand.

Legacy Reflection

Diligence and stewardship are the legacy of a godly wife. They are the evidence of her wisdom, the fruit of her faith, and the fragrance of her worship. She does not waste time. She redeems it. She does not fear lack. She walks in abundance. She does not chase after more—she multiplies what she has. Her hands are diligent. Her heart is peaceful. Her life is well-ordered. This is her power. This is her posture. This is her legacy.

Reflection

"Faithfulness is not a suggestion—it is the sacred standard of stewardship. In every assignment, every season, and every unseen sacrifice, the true steward is measured not by applause, but by unwavering obedience."

Chapter 12

Prayer Warrior: Interceding for Family and Destiny

"The effective, fervent prayer of a righteous woman avails much."
— James 5:16 (adapted)

Prayer Is Not Passive—It's Prophetic

The godly wife is not just a nurturer—she's a warrior. Her prayers are not just whispers of worry; they are declarations of destiny. She does not just hope for change, but she fights for it. Her intercession is not emotional. It is strategic.

Prayer is not a last resort; it is the first response. It acts as the altar where battles are won before they even begin. The godly wife understands that her authority in prayer does not rely on volume but is grounded in alignment with heaven.

"Whatever you bind on earth will be bound in heaven, and whatever you loose on earth will be loosed in heaven."
— Matthew 18:18

She doesn't just pray for comfort, but she prays for victory. She not only asks for peace, but she also declares triumph.

Strategic Prayer for Husband, Children, and Legacy

Intercession is intentional, not random. The godly wife prays with purpose. She covers her husband's mind, leadership, integrity, and calling. She speaks life into his identity, wisdom into his decisions, and strength into his spirit. She does not nag—she kneels. She does not criticize—she covers.

"*Her husband is known in the gates...*"
– Proverbs 31:23

She prays for her children with purpose. She declares protection over their bodies, purity over their hearts, and an intentional future. She does not just pray for safety. She prays for a spiritual legacy. She builds generational altars with her words. She plants seeds of destiny through her declarations. Her prayers serve as prophetic blueprints for her family's future.

"*I have no greater joy than to hear that my children walk in truth.*"
– 3 John 1:4

She does not just pray for what is—she prays for what will be.

Fasting and Spiritual Warfare

Fasting is not starvation; it is sanctification. It is the deliberate denial of the flesh to strengthen the voice of the Spirit. The godly wife uses fasting as a weapon of warfare, a tool of clarity, and a posture of surrender.

"*This kind does not go out except by prayer and fasting.*"
– Matthew 17:21

She fasts not to control or manipulate God, but to magnify and honor Him. She fasts to overcome barriers, silence doubts, and achieve breakthroughs. Her fasting is not just a ritual. On the contrary, it is a source of insight. Spiritual warfare is not showy; it requires discipline. A godly wife wears the whole armor of God every day. She does not battle her husband—she advocates for him. She does not fight her children. Instead, she prays for their future.

> *"For the weapons of our warfare are not carnal*
> *but mighty in God for pulling down strongholds."*
> – 2 Corinthians 10:4

She prays in the Spirit. She declares the Word. She worships through warfare. Her home becomes a battleground of breakthroughs, not breakdowns.

The Mantle of Intercession

The godly wife wears the mantle of intercession with honor. She is not just a woman of prayer; she is a woman of power. Her prayers change atmospheres, calm storms, and ignite movements. She does not wait for revival. On the contrary, she brings it forth in her closet. She does not fear the future. She shapes it with her faith. She doesn't retreat, but she rises.

> *"Call to Me and I will answer you, and tell you great and*
> *unsearchable things you do not know."*
> – Jeremiah 33:3

Her intercession serves not only for survival but also for strategy. She prays not only for comfort, but for conquest. She is not only a wife, but also a warrior.

Legacy Reflection

Prayer and fasting are the legacy of a godly wife. They are the fragrance of her faith, the fire of her warfare, and the foundation of her family's future. She does not just pray—she prevails. She does not just fast—she fights. She does not just hope—she heals. Her prayers are not quiet; they are catalytic. Her fasting is not empty, it is explosive. Her intercession is not ordinary; it is ordained. This is her power. This is her posture. This is her legacy.

Reflection

"When a righteous woman prays, she does not whisper into the wind—she strikes the heavens with fire. Her fervent cry is not noise; it is negotiation with God, and the earth must respond."

Chapter 13

Encourager and Builder: Speaking Life into Destiny

"The Sovereign Lord has given me a well-instructed tongue, to know the word that sustains the weary."
— Isaiah 50:4 (NIV)

Words Are Not Casual—They're Creative

In the kingdom, words are not merely communication; they are acts of creation. God spoke the world into existence, and the godly wife carries that same creative power through her words. Her words do not just describe reality; they shape it. Her voice is not only heard but also felt in the spiritual realm.

A godly wife is not just a speaker—she is a builder. Her encouragement is not flattery; it is fuel. Her affirmation is not emotional; it is prophetic. She speaks life into dry bones, destiny into delay, and legacy into the ordinary.

"The tongue has the power of life and death..."
— Proverbs 18:21

She does not waste words; she commands them. She does not mimic culture. She proclaims a kingdom.

Prophetic Affirmation and Legacy Language

Prophetic affirmation is not just hype; it is sacred. It has the power to see beyond the present moment and speak into the miracle. The godly wife affirms her husband not only for who he is but also for who he is becoming. She calls forth the king in him, even when he feels like just a servant. She speaks legacy into her children. She declares identity, purpose, and purity. She does not just say "I love you". On the contrary, she says, "You are chosen, called, and covered." Her words become generational seeds, sown into the soil of their spirits.

"Encourage one another daily..."
— Hebrews 3:13

Legacy language is purposeful. It is not reactive; it is revelatory. It represents the vocabulary of vision, the dialect of destiny, and the soundtrack of spiritual inheritance. She does not just affirm actions; she affirms existence. She does not just compliment, she commissions.

Building Up with Intentional Words

Intentional words are not random; they are meaningful. The godly wife chooses her words as a master builder selects bricks. She understands that each sentence can either build up or tear down. She speaks with purpose, not impulsively; she speaks with insight.

"She opens her mouth with wisdom,
and the teaching of kindness is on her tongue."
— Proverbs 31:26

She builds her husband's confidence with integrity. She shapes her children's character with truth. She fosters a peaceful atmosphere in her home. Her words are gentle; they are illuminating. Her tone is calm; it is sacred. She does not tear down with sarcasm—she builds up with sincerity. She does not nag—she nurtures. She does not criticize—she inspires. Her intentionality is not just emotional intelligence; it is spiritual stewardship.

The Ministry of Encouragement

Encouragement is not a personality trait—it is a calling. It is the power to uplift weary souls, reignite dormant dreams, and rebuild broken confidence. The godly wife becomes a source of hope, a fountain of affirmation, and a voice of revival.

"Therefore, encourage one another and build each other up..."
— 1 Thessalonians 5:11

She encourages not only when it is easy but also when it is crucial. She talks about life in the valley, not just on the mountaintop. Her encouragement is sincere; it is sacred. It is rooted in scripture, wrapped in grace, and given with strength. Her ministry is not on a stage; it is in her living room. Her pulpit is her prayer closet. Her platform is her kitchen table. Her legacy is written in the hearts of those she influences.

Legacy Reflection

Encouragement and affirmation are the legacy of a godly wife. They are the fragrance of her faith, the rhythm of her revelation, and the ministry of her words. She does not just speak—she shapes. She does not just affirm—she activates. She does not just build—she births destiny. Her words are not empty; they are eternal. Her tone is not casual; it is consecrated. Her voice is not ordinary; it is ordained. This is her power. This is her posture. This is her legacy.

Reflection

“When the Sovereign Lord instructs your tongue, your words become more than speech—they become sanctuary. A righteous voice, seasoned by heaven, carries the power to lift the weary, rebuke despair, and awaken purpose.”

Chapter 14

Modesty and Honor: Dressing and Living with Dignity

"Your beauty should not come from outward adornment... Rather, it should be that of your inner self, the unfading beauty of a gentle and quiet spirit, which is of great worth in God's sight."
– 1 Peter 3:3–4 (NIV)

Modesty Is Not Shame—It's Significance

In a culture that links exposure with empowerment, the godly wife sends a different message. Her modesty is not repression; it is revelation. It shows her understanding of worth, her reverence for God, and her commitment to kingdom identity. Modesty is not about hiding; it is about honoring. It is a sacred choice to dress and live in a way that reflects dignity, not distraction. It is not a rejection of beauty—it is a new definition of it.

"Charm is deceptive, and beauty is fleeting;
but a woman who fears the Lord is to be praised."
– Proverbs 31:30

She does not dress to attract attention—she dresses to express intention. Her clothing is not a costume; it is a covenant. It says, "I belong to God. I carry glory. I walk in purpose."

Modesty as a Message

Every outfit speaks. The godly wife understands that her wardrobe is a testimony. Trends do not determine her style—it is shaped by truth. She selects garments that reflect grace, not superficiality. She adorns herself with wisdom, not worldly approval. Modesty is not just about fabric—it is about focus. It shifts attention from the body to the spirit, from the external to the eternal. It says, "I am more than what you see—I am who God says I am."

"She is clothed with strength and dignity;
she can laugh at the days to come."
– Proverbs 31:25

Her humility is not insecurity; it is purposefulness. It is the quiet confidence of a woman who recognizes her worth and refuses to trade it for attention.

Honor in Public and Private

Honor is not just a virtue—it is a way of life. The godly wife acts with integrity whether she is seen or unseen. She doesn't perform for others—she lives for God. Her honor is not situational. It is spiritual.

In public, she carries herself gracefully. She speaks kindly and moves thoughtfully. She does not seek the spotlight—she reflects the light of Christ. In private, she respects her husband, shows patience with her children, and maintains her purity. She does not compromise; in secret, she dedicates herself. Her private life does not contradict her public witness; it affirms it.

"Whoever walks in integrity walks securely..."
– Proverbs 10:9

Honor is not just about reputation; it is about disclosure. It reveals the heart of a woman who fears the Lord, values her calling, and protects her legacy.

Dignity: The Fruit of Modesty and Honor

Dignity is the fragrance of a woman who walks with both modesty and honor. It embodies the quiet strength of someone who knows she is royalty. It reflects the posture of someone who refuses to be ordinary. It is the presence of someone who bears heaven's weight. The godly wife does not need to prove herself—she positions herself. She does not chase attention—she cultivates anointing. Her dignity is not pride; it is purity.

"Let your light so shine before men, that they may see your good works and glorify your Father in heaven."
– Matthew 5:16

She shines—not because she is flashy, but because she is loyal. Her modesty is her cover. Her honor is her shield. Her dignity is her statement.

Legacy Reflection

Modesty and honor define a godly wife. They show her reverence, resulting from her wisdom, and are the essence of her walk. She does not expose herself—she sets an example. She does not perform—she protects. She does not blend in. She witnesses. Her clothing signifies a covenant. Her posture reflects purity. Her presence emanates power. This is her message. This is her mantle. This is her legacy.

Reflection

"True beauty is not worn—it is woven. It flows from a spirit anchored in grace, a heart quieted by truth, and a soul that reflects heaven's worth. What fades in mirrors is nothing compared to what shines in God's sight."

Chapter 15

Joyful Motherhood: Nurturing the Next Generation

"Her children arise and call her blessed;
her husband also, and he praises her."
— Proverbs 31:28 (NIV)

Motherhood Is Ministry

Motherhood is more than a biological role. It is a spiritual calling. The godly wife recognizes that nurturing the next generation is not a side task. On the contrary, it is key to leaving a kingdom legacy. Whether through birth, adoption, mentorship, or spiritual discipleship, she embraces the mantle of motherhood with joy, not just duty.

Joyful motherhood is not about being perfect. Instead, it is about being present. It embodies the sacred rhythm of loving, guiding, and uplifting children into their divine identity. It is the ministry of shaping hearts, developing character, and planting vision.

"Train up a child in the way he should go,
and when he is old, he will not depart from it."
— Proverbs 22:6

She does not just raise children; she aims and directs arrows. She not only controls behaviors but also guides destiny.

Spiritual Motherhood and Mentoring

Spiritual motherhood is not limited by age or biology. It is powered by wisdom and compassion. The godly wife acts as a spiritual mother to younger women, mentees, and even her peers. She shares truth, testimony, and irrefutable grace.

"Likewise, teach the older women to be reverent... to teach what is good. Then they can urge the younger women..."
– Titus 2:3–4

She mentors with humility, not hierarchy. She listens with empathy, not ego. She disciplines with Scripture, not opinion. Her life becomes a classroom, her words become curriculum, and her love becomes a legacy. Spiritual motherhood isn't about control — it's about cultivation. It's the art of drawing out destiny, not dictating direction.

Raising Children with Vision and Grace

Children are not just bodies to feed—they are spirits to nurture. The godly wife raises her children with vision, not merely rules. She speaks destiny over them, prays purpose into them, and models grace before them. She does not just discipline—she disciples. She does not just correct—she calls forth. Her parenting is prophetic, not reactive. She sees beyond the tantrum to the testimony. She sees beyond the mess to the mantle.

"I will pour out My Spirit on your offspring,
and My blessing on your descendants."
– Isaiah 44:3

Grace in parenting means choosing restoration over rage, connection over control, and presence over perfection. It involves apologizing when needed, affirming often, and grounding everything in love. She raises children who know God, not just rules. Her children walk in purpose, not just performance. They carry legacy, and not just lineage.

Joy in the Journey

Joyful motherhood is not the absence of struggle. On the contrary, it is the act of surrender. It is laughing through laundry, worshiping amid weariness, and praying despite pressure. It is choosing gratitude over grumbling, and grace over guilt.

"Children are a heritage from the Lord,
offspring a reward from Him."
– Psalm 127:3

She celebrates small victories. She honors sacred moments. She embraces chaos as part of the calling. Her joy is not shallow — it is spiritual. It flows from knowing that every diaper changed, every prayer whispered, and every tear wiped is building eternity.

Her motherhood is not mundane—it is miraculous.

Legacy Reflection

Joyful motherhood is the legacy of a godly wife. It is the fragrance of her faith, the rhythm of her grace, and the ministry of her heart. She does not just parent—she prophesies. She does not just manage—she mentors. She does not just survive, she sanctifies. Her children are not just raised, they are released. Her home is not just busy, it is blessed. Her motherhood is not just natural, it is supernatural. This is her power. This is her posture. This is her legacy.

Reflection

"A woman of legacy is not just remembered—she is honored. Her children stand with pride in their voices, her husband speaks her praise, because her life speaks louder than words and her love created altars in their hearts."

PART IV: TRAITS THAT REFLECT KINGDOM AUTHORITY

Chapter 16

Boldness in Faith: Standing Firm in Truth

"Be on your guard; stand firm in the faith;
be courageous; be strong."
– 1 Corinthians 16:13 (NIV)

Courage in Culture and Conviction

In a world that values compromise over conviction, the godly wife rises with courage. Her boldness is not arrogance; it is alignment. She is not loud for attention—she is firm for truth. She does not follow trends—she bows to truth. Boldness in faith is not about being confrontational; it is about being consistent. It's the sacred strength to live by God's standards even when culture mocks them. It's the courage to say "no" to what's popular and "yes" to what's eternal.

"Do not conform to the pattern of this world,
but be transformed by the renewing of your mind."
– Romans 12:2

She refuses to dilute her convictions to fit in. On the contrary, she deepens them to stand out. Her courage is not aggressive. It is compassionate. She does not fight people. Instead, she fights for purity, purpose, and legacy.

Speaking Truth with Love

Truth without love is harsh. Love without truth is hollow. The godly wife walks in both. She speaks truth not to shame—but to shine. She corrects not to condemn—but to call forth. Her words are not daggers—they are declarations.

"Instead, speaking the truth in love, we will grow to become in every respect the mature body of Him who is the head, that is, Christ."
— Ephesians 4:15

She does not shy away from difficult conversations—she faces them with humility and respect. She does not weaponize scripture—she uses it wisely. Her voice becomes a channel for healing rather than hostility. Speaking truth with love involves knowing when to stay silent, when to speak, and how to add grace to every word. It means favoring restoration over revenge, clarity over faultfinding, and conviction over comfort.

Boldness Is Not Loud—It's Loyal

Boldness is not about how loud you are. It is about loyalty to God. The godly wife is bold because she's secure. She does not fear rejection. She respects righteousness. She does not seek applause. Instead, she exudes authority. Her boldness is not reckless. It is grounded. It comes from intimacy with God, not insecurity about others. She stands firm not because she is fearless, but because she is full of faith.

"The righteous are as bold as a lion."
— Proverbs 28:1

She does not shrink back, but she steps forward. She does not apologize for truth—she affirms it with grace. Her boldness becomes a beacon for her children, a shield for her husband, and a standard for her generation.

Boldness in the Everyday

Boldness is not just for pulpits. It is for parenting, marriage, and those moments when compromise whispers and conviction must shout. The godly wife is bold when she prays over her family, guards her home, and speaks life into broken places. She is bold when she says "no" to gossip, "yes" to holiness, and "not today" to the enemy's lies. Her boldness is not dramatic, but it is daily. It is the quiet strength of a woman who knows who she is and whose she is.

"Have I not commanded you? Be strong and courageous. Do not be afraid; do not be discouraged, for the Lord your God will be with you wherever you go."

– Joshua 1:9

Her boldness is not just for battle. It is for building. It forms the foundation of her legacy —the fragrance of her faith and the fire of her witness.

Legacy Reflection

Confidence and boldness in faith are the heritage of a godly wife. It is the proof of her conviction, the result of her intimacy, and her purposeful stance. She does not merely believe — she builds. She does not only speak — she sanctifies. She does not simply stand — she shines. Her courage is not cultural — it is divine. Her truth is not trendy — it is eternal. Her love is not passive. Instead, it is prophetic. This is her strength. This is her stance. This is her legacy.

Reflection

“Faith is not passive; it is a stance of battle. To stand firm means refusing to retreat; to be brave is to speak truth when silence seems safer, and to be strong is to carry the weight of a legacy when others give up. Guard your ground, for heaven supports the bold.”

Chapter 17

Vision and Purpose: Living Beyond the Moment

"Write the vision and make it plain on tablets, that he may run who reads it."
— Habakkuk 2:2 (NKJV)

Living Beyond the Moment

Circumstances do not constrain the godly wife —she is driven by calling. She does not live reactively; she lives prophetically. Her life is not guided by emotion, but by vision. She looks beyond the moment because she walks with the One who holds eternity.

Vision is not fantasy—it is spiritual foresight. It is the ability to see what God sees, even when it hasn't yet manifested. Purpose is not performance—it is a divine assignment. It is the reason she was created, the legacy she is called to release, and the impact she is destined to multiply.

"Where there is no vision, the people perish..."
— Proverbs 29:18 (KJV)

She does not survive seasons. On the contrary, she manages them. She not only endures change but also welcomes it with clarity and courage.

Understanding Seasons and Assignments

Every season has a specific purpose. The godly wife recognizes the difference between preparation and promotion, pruning and planting, warfare and worship. She does not rush through seasons; she respects them.

"*To everything there is a season,*
a time for every purpose under heaven."
– Ecclesiastes 3:1

She knows that winter is not punishment; it is preparation. Spring is not just about beauty; it is birthing. Summer is not merely abundance; it is stewardship. Autumn is not just a transition—it is a transformation.

Assignments are not always glamorous and often go unnoticed. She may be called to serve quietly, work behind the scenes, or build in the background. Yet, she knows that obedience in every season opens the door to abundance later. She asks not, "How long will this last?" but "What am I called to release here?"

Dreaming with God

Dreaming with God is not wishful thinking—it is a prophetic partnership. The godly wife does not dream based on her limitations but on His guidance. She does not ask for what is safe; she asks for what is sacred.

"*Now to Him who is able to do immeasurably*
more than all we ask or imagine..."
– Ephesians 3:20

She dreams of legacy, not just lifestyle. She dreams of impact, not just income. She dreams of generations walking in truth, nations touched by grace, and ministries born from her living room. Her dreams are not selfish; they are strategic. They are not shallow; they are spiritual. She dreams with open hands, a surrendered heart, and a pen ready to write the vision. Dreaming with God means asking, "What do You want to do through me?" and having the boldness to believe He will.

Vision as a Mantle, Purpose as a Map

Vision is the mantle she wears—purpose is the map she follows. The godly wife does not wander—she walks with wisdom. She does not chase trends; she follows truth. Her life is not random—it is a revelation. She builds with eternity in mind. She speaks with legacy on her tongue. She moves with heaven in her heart.

"Many are the plans in a person's heart,
but it is the Lord's purpose that prevails."
— Proverbs 19:21

Her vision is clear. It is vivid. Her purpose is to be active. It is powerful. She lives beyond the moment because she is rooted in her mission.

Legacy Reflection

Vision and purpose shape the legacy of a godly wife. They serve as proof of her intimacy, born from her obedience, and the flame of her faith. She does not just dream; she makes disciples. She does not just plan; she prophesies. She does not just move; she multiplies. Her seasons are sacred. Her assignments are strategic. Her dreams are divine. This is her power. This is her posture. This is her legacy.

Reflection

"A vision unwritten is a victory delayed. When God speaks, clarity is your assignment—write it boldly, plainly, and prophetically, so that those called to run with it won't stumble in the *fog of* ambiguity."

Chapter 18

Unity and Partnership: Co-Laboring in Ministry and Marriage

*"Two are better than one,
because they have a good return for their labor."*
— Ecclesiastes 4:9 (NIV)

Marriage Is Not Just Romance—It's Kingdom Partnership

The godly wife recognizes that marriage is more than just an emotional bond. It is a spiritual partnership. She is not just a companion—she is a co-laborer. Her union is not solely for comfort but also for calling. Together, she and her husband form a ministry team —a legacy-building force and a reflection of Christ and the Church.

Unity is not about uniformity. It is about collaboration. It represents the sacred rhythm where two distinct callings come together harmoniously for a shared divine purpose. It doesn't mean losing individuality; instead, it is about aligning our purpose.

"Therefore, what God has joined together, let no one separate."
— Mark 10:9

She does not compete with her husband. She completes him. She does not resist his leadership. On the contrary, she supports it. Their partnership is not perfect, but it is strong.

Building Together in Purpose

Purpose is not a solo pursuit. It is a shared mission. The godly wife builds with her husband. She stands beside him. She prays over his vision, offers her gifts, and amplifies their influence. She recognizes that her role is not secondary. On the contrary, it is strategic.

"Unless the Lord builds the house, the builders labor in vain."
— Psalm 127:1

They build a home that reflects heaven. They establish a ministry that heals. They create a legacy that endures beyond them. Their unity is not just emotional; it is missional.

Building together involves sharing burdens, celebrating breakthroughs, and managing resources wisely. It means dreaming as a team, discerning together, and discipling one another. She doesn't just support his calling—she pursues her own. Together, they become a powerful force for the kingdom.

Navigating Roles and Callings

Roles in marriage are not fixed—they unfold through prayer, purpose, and seasons. The godly wife recognizes that her calling might differ from her husband's—but it is just as divine. She does not shrink to conform; instead, she shines to fulfill.

"There are different kinds of gifts,
but the same Spirit distributes them."
— 1 Corinthians 12:4

She may be called to teach, write, lead, nurture, or intercede. Her gifts are not in competition—they are in harmony. She respects her husband's role while embracing her own. She does not lose herself in marriage—she finds a deeper expression of her identity.

Navigating roles means communicating clearly, honoring with humility, and adjusting gracefully. It means asking, "How can we serve together?" not "Who leads louder?" It means understanding seasons—when one is directed to lead and the other to support. It involves honoring each other's roles, not resenting them.

Unity Is Warfare Against Division

Unity is more than emotional harmony. It is spiritual warfare. The enemy fears a united marriage more than a gifted individual. The godly wife fights for unity through prayer, forgiveness, and intentional connection.

> *"Make every effort to keep the unity of the Spirit through the bond of peace."*
> – Ephesians 4:3

She does not let offense linger. She prevents silence from becoming separation. She starts healing conversations, builds intimacy, and safeguards the partnership. Her unity with her husband acts as a shield for her children, a platform for ministry, and a testimony to the world.

Legacy Reflection

Unity and partnership are the legacy of a godly wife. They serve as proof of her wisdom, rooted in her humility and faith. She does not just marry—she ministers. She does not merely support, she strengthens. She not only follows but also collaborates. Her marriage is not simply romantic; it is redemptive. Her partnership is not only emotional; it is eternal. Her unity is not just peaceful; it is powerful. This is her power. This is her posture. This is her legacy.

Reflection

"Kingdom impact multiplies through covenant alignment. When two walk as one—vision linked, labor shared—the harvest is not just doubled; it is divinely accelerated. Unity isn't addition; it's exponential return."

Chapter 19

Resilience and Endurance: Thriving Through Trials

"Blessed is she who has believed
that the Lord would fulfill His promises to her."
— Luke 1:45 (adapted)

Trials Are Not the End—They Are the Training

The godly wife recognizes that trials are not interruptions. On the contrary, they are invitations. They call her to grow deeper, stand stronger, and trust deeply and more fully. She does not see hardship as abandonment—she perceives it as alignment. Her resilience is not denial. Instead, it is divine determination.

Resilience is not the absence of pain. On the contrary, it is the strength to persevere. It is the sacred power to keep moving forward when the path is unclear, to keep believing when the breakthrough is delayed, and to keep loving when the heart feels exhausted.

"Consider it pure joy... whenever you face trials of many kinds,
because you know that the testing of your faith produces
perseverance."
— James 1:2–3

She does not just survive storms. She sings in them. She does not just endure seasons. She thrives through them.

Overcoming Weariness and Disappointment

Weariness is real, but not necessarily final. Disappointment may visit, but it does not stay. The godly wife learns to cast her cares, not carry them. She lays down the weight of unmet expectations and puts on the garment of praise.

> "*Come to Me, all you who are weary and burdened, and I will give you rest.*"
> – Matthew 11:28

She does not pretend to be strong. She seeks strength. She does not numb the pain. Instead, she names it before God. Her healing begins with honesty. Her endurance is born in intimacy. Disappointment is not a detour—it is a doorway. It leads her to deeper dependence, clearer vision, and refined faith. She learns to say, "Even here, God is good. Even now, I will trust." She does not let weariness define her—she lets worship revive her.

Endurance Is Not Passive–It is Prophetic

Endurance is not just waiting; it is fighting. It is the spiritual discipline of standing firm when everything urges you to sit down. It is the prophetic stance of believing when everything encourages you to give up.

> "*Let us run with endurance the race that is set before us, fixing our eyes on Jesus...*"
> – Hebrews 12:1–2

The godly wife endures not because she is stubborn, but because she has surrendered. She does not stop calming her soul. She does not panic; she prays. Her endurance is not emotional; it is eternal. She perseveres in marriage, motherhood, and ministry, not because it is easy, but because it is sacred. She understands that each challenge is shaping her testimony, every delay is strengthening her reliance, and each tear is nourishing her legacy.

Joy in the Journey

Joy isn't the absence of struggle. It welcomes the presence of God. The godly wife finds joy not only in the destination but also in the daily journey. She laughs while doing laundry, worships amid weariness, and dances despite disappointment.

"The joy of the Lord is your strength."
– Nehemiah 8:10

Her joy is not superficial; it is sacred. It arises from revelation, not reaction. It comes from knowing that God is with her, for her, and working through her. She finds joy in small victories, sacred moments, and silent prayers. Her journey is not perfect, but it is purposeful. Her happiness is not loud — but it endures. She does not wait for joy — she walks in it!

Legacy Reflection

Resilience and endurance define a godly wife's legacy. They demonstrate her strength, born from surrender, and embody her faith. She goes beyond mere endurance to empower others. She surpasses survival to sanctify her surroundings. Her walk is also an act of worship. Her fatigue evolves into wisdom, and her disappointments shape her destiny. Her journey evolves into joy. This is her power, her stance, her legacy.

Reflection

"She is not blessed because she waited—she is blessed because she believed. Faith made her womb a sanctuary *for* promise, and her trust unlocked the timing *of* heaven."

Chapter 20

Legacy and Impact: Becoming a Crown of Glory

"Her children arise and call her blessed; her husband also, and he praises her... a woman who fears the Lord is to be praised."
— Proverbs 31:28, 30 (NIV)

Legacy Is Not What You Leave—It's What You Launch

The godly wife doesn't just live for today—she lives for future generations. Her impact is not measured by applause but by the legacy she leaves behind. She is not simply a wife, she's a wellspring. She is not just a mother, she's a multiplier. Her life becomes a harvest for legacy, a plan for blessing, and a crown of glory in the hands of her Redeemer.

Legacy is not just about possessions. It is about patterns. It is the spiritual DNA she passes down to her children, her marriage, her ministry, and her community. It includes the prayers she said, the wisdom she shared, and the love she has given and lived out.

"The righteous lead blameless lives;
blessed are their children after them."
— Proverbs 20:7

She does not just raise children, she aims arrows. She does not just build a home—she creates a legacy.

Multiplying Influence Through Generations

The godly wife multiplies. She increases peace in her home, wisdom in her words, and grace in her relationships. Her influence extends beyond her lifetime—it resonates through generations. She mentors daughters, guides younger women, and demonstrates kingdom living for all who meet her.

"One generation shall commend Your works to another, and shall declare Your mighty acts."
— Psalm 145:4

Her legacy is intentional, not accidental. She plants scripture in her children's hearts, speaks destiny into her husband's spirit, and creates pathways for others to find purpose. Her life becomes a living altar, a generational well, and a prophetic voice. She multiplies not through effort—but through surrender. Not through control—but through consecration. Her legacy is not loud, but enduring.

The Godly Wife as a Kingdom Multiplier

The godly wife multiplies the kingdom. She takes what God provides and expands it. She increases love, truth, and influence. She turns meals into ministry, conversations into counsel, and everyday moments into eternal movements.

"She considers a field and buys it;
out of her earnings she plants a vineyard."
— Proverbs 31:16

She contributes through prayer, active engagement, and collaborative efforts. Her home serves as a place of restoration. Her marriage demonstrates commitment to shared goals. Her approach to motherhood emphasizes growth and development. She not only adds value but also enhances strategic vision. She provides foundational support for ministry initiatives and fosters their growth. She upholds the legacy by empowering future generations. Her influence extends beyond age, circumstance, or position, guided by dedication, strong relationships, and insight.

Becoming a Crown of Glory

A crown is more than a symbol. It is a declaration. The godly wife becomes a crown of glory—not because she is perfect, but because she is faithful. Her life reflects the beauty of holiness, the strength of surrender, and the radiance of righteousness.

"In that day the Lord Almighty will be a glorious crown,
a beautiful wreath for the remnant of His people."
– Isaiah 28:5

She wears dignity like a robe. Like a queen, she walks wisely. She speaks with grace like a prophetess. Her crown is not made of gold—it is made of glory. She does not just remember, she is revered. She is not just honored, she is multiplied. Her legacy becomes a beacon for generations to come.

Legacy Reflection

Legacy and impact are the final fragrance of a godly wife. They are the evidence of her obedience, the fruit of her faith, and the crown of her consecration. She does not just live—she launches. She does not just influence—she ignites. She does not just bless—she builds. Her life is not just a testimony—it is a template. Her home is not just peaceful, it is prophetic. Her legacy is not just remembered, it is reproduced. This is her power. This is her posture. This is her crown of glory.

Reflection

“She is not honored for beauty that fades, but for reverence that endures. Her children rise with gratitude, her husband with praise, because her fear of the Lord shaped a home where love was a legacy and worship was woven into every wall.”

Conclusion

You have journeyed through pages that do more than instruct—they guide and illuminate. These vital traits are not a checklist to gain approval, but a compass pointing toward divine alignment. They are not burdens to carry, but blessings to embody. Each trait reflects God's heart for womanhood, marriage, and legacy.

Being a joyful and godly wife is not about perfection. On the contrary, it is about faithfulness. It means waking each day with a heart rooted in grace, a spirit surrendered to God, and a will resolved to love deeply, serve joyfully, and walk humbly. It also involves understanding that your influence goes beyond your home, echoing through generations, shaping destinies, and transforming atmospheres.

You are not just a wife, you are a worshipper, a warrior, and a wellspring of wisdom. Your joy is not dependent on circumstances; it is rooted in your covenant. Your strength does not come from striving but from surrendering. Your beauty is not in adornment but in the quiet power of a spirit that fully trusts God.

As you close this book, may you open your heart wider to the sacred calling you carry. Let these traits take root, not just in your habits, but in your identity. Let them shape your prayers, your posture, and your presence. And when the world tries to redefine your worth, return to the Word that never changes.

You are the daughter of the King. A builder of homes. A keeper of peace. A vessel of joy. A reflection of God's glory. Walk boldly. Love deeply. Serve faithfully. And never forget—your life, lived in godliness and joy, is a sermon the world cannot ignore.

Now go, live boldly, and carry on the legacy.

— *Dr. David Scott*

www.ingramcontent.com/pod-product-compliance
Lightning Source LLC
LaVergne TN
LVHW051012080826
845145LV00009B/2576